THE BOOK OF JOB

THE
BOOK OF JOB

BY

NORMAN H. SNAITH, M.A.

Tutor in Old Testament Languages and Literature,
Wesley College, Headingley, Leeds

THE EPWORTH PRESS

(EDGAR C. BARTON)

25-35 City Road, London, E.C.1

Made in Great Britain

I

THE ANALYSIS OF THE BOOK

1. *The Prologue, i, ii*

JOB is a wealthy Edomite sheikh of long ago, the greatest and most prosperous of them all, a man of blameless piety, scrupulous, even ultra-scrupulous in every slightest duty, perfect, upright and devout. Jehovah Himself testifies to his unswerving integrity, unique among the sons of men, but the Satan challenges this statement in the midst of the heavenly court. Job is but a time-server. Strip him of his wealth, kill his children, and he will renounce God with the rest. And so the Satan is permitted to deprive Job of everything, possessions, servants, children, but not to touch Job himself. Bedawi raids begin, and lightnings and storm-winds complete the destitution, but Job in his poverty is as devout as Job with his wealth.

The heavenly court gathers again, with God still sure of Job's integrity and the Satan still unbelieving. Now the Satan is permitted to smite Job with a loathsome 'leprosy' (probably ecthyma), in which the sufferer is covered from head to foot with raw and itching ulcers. Job's wife breaks under the strain, but Job remains steadfastly devout.

The last three verses of ii tell of the visit of Job's three friends, who hear of his misfortunes and come to comfort him. They sit with him in the dust for seven days and nights, silently, but with every manifestation of extreme grief.

2. *Job's Soliloquies, iii and xxix–xxxi*

There are two. In the first (iii) Job curses the day of his birth. Why was I ever born, or, being born, why did I ever live? In death there is rest and forgetfulness for all, rich and poor, wicked and weary, small and great. Why does God hedge in with life those who long for death? In the second soliloquy (xxix–xxxi), Job contrasts his former magnificence with his present wretchedness. Formerly all men respected him and sought his counsel; now even youngsters deride him and base men spurn him from their path. The God who once gave him prosperity is now silent to his cry. Job reiterates his uprightness; he has manifested every virtue both in thought and deed. If he has erred in aught, then he is prepared for the direst penalties. If only he knew what was the charge against him, then he could answer it, and all would be well.

3. *First Cycle of Speeches, iv–xiv*

Eliphaz (iv, v) rebukes Job, but with all tenderness. It is strange that one who has comforted others should himself break down under his own troubles. Job knows very well that only the wicked perish. God, in His wisdom and might, overthrows all the devices of crafty men. The man whom God chastens is blessed. It is but for a season; his end is a ripe old age and a peaceful death. Job's reply (vi, vii) is a criticism of God's ways with men. He uses His power tyrannically, and gives man no chance. Job's friends are 'Job's comforters'. Man's lot is one of misery. The speech concludes with a bitter parody of Psalm viii. 4.

Bildad (viii) holds that God is righteous and can do no wrong. If Job is truly righteous, then all he has to do is to appeal to God, and he will soon be restored to increased prosperity. The ancients knew this, and it is presumptuous to deride them. The doom of the wicked is certain, and the upright man will be upheld.

Job (ix, x) seizes on the idea of God being righteous. Yes, God is righteous, but 'righteous' means 'being in the right' (cf. Exodus ix. 27; Job xl. 8). Of course God is always in the right. He is too powerful for a mortal to put Him in the wrong. He crushes all opposition, and cares only to exert His sovereign will. I will protest to the end, come what may, even though there is no umpire to see fair play. Job ends by saying that he believes God meant all along to destroy him.

Zophar rebukes Job (xi). God is wise, and if Job will repent of his iniquity, he will soon know blessedness again. Job ends the cycle (xii–xiv) by mocking at the wisdom of his friends. He wants to have this matter out with God. Let Him lay aside His *mysterium tremendum*. Let Him speak plainly and allow me to have my say. But God gives me no chance. Man's day is short, fading as wild flowers fade. Let him make the most of it. The end is oblivion.

4. Second Cycle of Speeches, xv–xxi

Here the three friends do little more than each in his turn to reiterate the orthodox theory, Eliphaz (xv), Bildad (xviii), and Zophar (xx). Job's reply to Eliphaz (xvi, xvii) is that he could talk like that if he was in Eliphaz's place. As it is, God is determinedly hostile to him in spite of his innocence. Then Job suddenly turns from his friends to God (xvi. 19), appealing to the God who must be, against the God of orthodoxy, but he soon (xvi. 22) reverts to a former theme that his only hope is the grave. His reply to Bildad (xix) is that God definitely has dealt unfairly with him. Though all have forsaken him, Job is sure that he will be vindicated at last. Job's reply to Zophar (xxi) is a flat contradiction. It is a matter of experience that the wicked live long and happily. To say anything else is to fly in the face of the facts.

5. *Third Cycle of Speeches*, *xxii–xxvii*

Eliphaz changes his attitude. God is a strict Arbiter, exactly and precisely just. Job therefore must be a great sinner. Let him repent and all will be well. Job's reply (xxiii, xxiv. 1) is a plea that God will allow Himself to be accessible, or will allow a settling day occasionally to put things straight. In xxiv. 2–end, he continues with a description of the prosperity of wicked men contrasted with the trials of the righteous. The chapter has been subjected to rigorous criticism, the last verse only being universally admitted to be genuine. Some objections are due to the chapter being largely in tristichs instead of the usual distichs. Hence Merx objects to verses 9–24, which he says are a substitute for a too-vigorous tirade; Bickell to 5–8, 10–24; Duhm, who has applied his devastating versification theories to Jeremiah and Isaiah, omits 1–4, 5–12, 13–18a, 18b–24 as an intruding poem in four stanzas. Peake and Gray hold that the number of tristichs is greatly exaggerated, and do not object to the variation.

8

Gray omits only 10*a* and 11*a*, transposing 9 to follow 3, and 14*c* to follow 15. If 18–21 are to stand, then Job is quoting previous speakers in order to refute them. Gray allows this, but not Budde and Peake, who excise them, and also 9 and 24. Grill objects to 5–9 and 14–21; Siegfried to 13–24.

xxv–xxvii is confused. Bildad has five verses only allotted to him. Zophar has no third speech, and Job speaks at great length. xxvi, 5–14 is very like Bildad's sentiments, and much of xxvii contradicts what Job says elsewhere. The most probable reconstruction is that of Peake: Bildad, xxv. 2, 3, xxvi. 5–14; Zophar, xxvii. 13–23 (possibly also 7–10, though 8–10 may be a gloss); Job's reply to Bildad, xxvi. 2–4, xxvii. 2–6, 11, 12. Peake and Strahan think another too-vigorous speech has been excised between verses 11 and 12. Perhaps xxv. 4–6 is a gloss, based on xv. 14–16. There are many other reconstructions, the chief being by Gray, Duhm, Bickell, Budde, Sellin, Marshall and Ley.

This leaves xxix–xxxi as Job's reply to Zophar and the conclusion of all the dialogues. They can only formally be regarded as part of the dialogue. They ignore the three friends altogether, and are a soliloquy comparable to iii.

6. *Poem on Wisdom, xxviii*

This is generally regarded as an insertion, though its style is equal to that of the original author. In so far as it has its place in the completed work, it demonstrates the futility of man's questionings, since God alone holds the key to all mysteries. For man,

Wisdom means bowing in humble reverence before God and doing what is right.

Either the chapter is an excerpt, or (Duhm) the refrain 'Whence cometh wisdom . . .' (12, 20) should stand also at the beginning. It is customary to regard verse 28 as an addition, but we do not see this necessity.

7. *The Elihu Speeches, xxxii–xxxvii*

These are an interpolation after the completion of the rest of the book. The writer was less competent, commenting on the dialogues, substantially as we have them now. Nothing before or after refers to Elihu or to anything he says. Particularly there is no reference to him either in Prologue or Epilogue. True, he has his own introduction, but it is prosy and verbose compared to i, ii. The speeches add nothing to what has gone before, and destroy the effect of what follows. The author of ii–xiv, xxix–xxxi, xxxviii, xxxix is far too great an artist to do that. If the speeches were not there, they would never be missed, and the book would be all the better. The style is different, and poorer. The interpolator is familiar with the style of the dialogues, and in part copies it, but the proportions of key-words is different. E.g. the three names for God, El, Eloah, Shaddai, occur nineteen, six, six times respectively in the Elihu speeches as against thirty-six, thirty-five, twenty-five in the rest of the Book. In the dialogues *ani* is found for 'I' fifteen times as against *anoki* eleven times, but in the Elihu speeches the instances are nine against two. There is less use of archaic forms of particles and suffixes. This archaic flavour is a characteristic of the original author, as if agreeing with the ancient setting of his tale. There are seventy-nine such archaisms in the rest of Job, nine in the Elihu speeches, and 164 in all the remainder of the Old Testament. The brilliancy of the style is missing. Elihu is tautologous, trite, and often futile (see especially the vapid reiteration of xxxii). Budde disagrees with this last, and claims that the difference in style is due to the interpolation of some thirty verses and to corruptions of the text. The verses which Budde would omit are 2–5, 11–12, 15–17. We do not find that these excise the tautologous couplets.

Budde takes these speeches seriously, and finds in them the author's solution. Job's sin was hidden spiritual pride, and the sufferings were to bring this to light. Elihu's function is to make this clear to Job. Budde's view creates more difficulties than it solves. Elihu refers to pride twice only, xxxiii. 17 and xxxvi. 9. Further, the theory does not agree with the absolute integrity on which the Prologue goes out of its way to insist. Job says it was God who convinced him of his error. What of the Jehovah speeches if the *dénouement* is in what Elihu says?

Cornill agrees with Budde, and stresses the educative function of suffering. Another suggestion is that the author made Elihu his butt. More recently Peters (1928) has defended the authenticity both of xxviii and of the Elihu speeches. Sellin, Bauer and Kamphausen all think the speeches to be a later addition by the original author, who had changed his ideas and whose hand (apparently) has lost its cunning. Box suggests that the author left them incomplete, thus accounting for the differences and the less elegant style.

8. *The Jehovah Speeches and Job's Recantations, xxxviii– xlii.* 6

Probably there was originally one Jehovah speech which consisted of xxxviii, xxxix with xl. 8–14; and one submission from Job, xl. 2–5 and xlii. 2–3, 5–6. Jehovah asks Job in a series of rhetorical questions what he knows of the great divine plan of creation and government, the mighty works in heaven above and the kindly providence to bird and beast on earth below. Job's reply is that he has spoken without knowledge, hearsay has now become sight, and he repents in sackcloth and ashes. So Peake, A. R. Gordon, and (partly) Gray.

The second Jehovah speech (xl. 15–xli. 34) is thus regarded as an interpolation. The style is better than that of the Elihu speeches, but not up to the standard of the original author. The descriptions are longer, and deal with the anatomy of the creatures rather than with their habits; the creatures are Egyptian or mythological, but not actual; if they are real, then the descriptions are exaggerated, which is not the case in the earlier speech; the questions are largely absent. Further, Job has already thrown up his case, and the second speech comes 'perilously near to nagging' (Peake). So Peake, Gray, Oesterley and Robinson, and Rowley (in *A Companion to the Bible*, 1939).

Other opinions are Cheyne, Van Hoonacker, Bertie, and Baumgärtel, who reject the whole section xxxviii– xlii. 6 as secondary. Hans Schmidt rejects all but xl. 1–4. Hölscher adopts the generally accepted position, but rejects xxxix. 13–18 in addition to the normal xl. 15–xli. 34. This involves the rejection of the description of the Ostrich as well as those of the Hippopotamus and the Crocodile. The objection to this is that the description of the ostrich is similar to that of the other creatures in the first speech and in marked contrast to the anatomical accounts of the other two.

The usually accepted identifications of the beasts of the second Jehovah speech are that they are Egyptian creatures, the hippopotamus and the crocodile. So Peake, Gray, and Oesterley and Robinson. On the other hand, Cheyne, Toy, Gunkel and Rowley hold to a mythological interpretation, Behemoth and Leviathan being both 'incarnations' of the great sea-monster, the Babylonian Tiamat, or the Hebrew Rahab. This latter explanation is, in our view, much to be preferred. It avoids the criticisms of exaggeration, and the Egyptian characteristics are accounted for by the age-old identification of Rahab with Egypt the oppressor (e.g. Isaiah xxx. 7, li. 9 f.).

9. *The Epilogue, xlii. 7–end*

Jehovah censures the three friends in that they have not spoken right of Him, and commends Job in that he has spoken that which was right. Job intercedes for them. They are pardoned, and Job is restored to a double prosperity.

Peake's opinion is that the author took an earlier Book of Job (some say from a *Volksbuch*), and replaced the original speeches with a dialogue of his own. He finds it difficult to accept xlii. 7, 8 as a true description of the dialogues as we have them now. So also Sellin, Duhm and Franks (in Peake's *Commentary*). On the other hand Gray, Dhorme and Hölscher favour a common authorship of prologue, dialogue and epilogue. Certainly the prologue with its insistence on Job's complete innocence is essential to the whole book, and we see no other means of achieving a happy ending when no real life after death is envisaged. Any demonstration of felicity must come in this world and it must be in the things of this world. Gray finds no stylistic differences in the prologue and epilogue beyond what would be inevitable for prose as against verse.

10. *Baumgärtel's Theory*

Baumgärtel limits the original work of the author, apart from the question of prologue and epilogue, to the first cycle of speeches and to a monologue from Job of which the fragments are to be found in xvi, xix, xxiii and xxxi. To this add the first Jehovah speech and Job's recantation, i.e. xxxviii, xxxix, xl. 8–14 with xl. 2–5, xlii. 2–3, 5–6. This limits Job's words to protestations of his innocence and to criticism of God's arbitrary use of His power. It enables xlii. 7, 8 to be retained as a reasonably just judgement of the relative merits of the speeches of Job and his friends. Job says nothing particularly outrageous in the first cycle of speeches, and he covers substantially the ground with which later Jehovah deals. The question of Job's guilt is not raised apart from xi. 6c, 14, and thus the poem keeps within the bounds of the prologue.

We ourselves are in agreement with Baumgärtel

except that we would find Job's monologue in iii and xxix–xxxi. One advantage of some such theory as this is that the difference in excellence between the first cycle of speeches and the other two cycles is thus accounted for. We hold iii, iv–xiv, xxix–xxxi, xxxviii, xxxix, xl. 8–14, and xl. 2–5, xliii. 5–6 to be much superior to the rest of the Book in style, elegance and matter, and that these sections form a complete whole. We suggest also that the three friends themselves may well have been an addendum to the original scheme, though, if so, this must have been made by the same author at a later date. This involves the excision of three verses at the end of the prologue, ii. 11–13, and three from the beginning of the epilogue, xlii. 7–9. It is remarkable how the remainder holds together— namely, i–ii. 10, iii and xxix–xxxi; xxxviii–xxxix with xl. 8–14; xl. 2–5 and xliii. 2–3, 5–6; xlii. 10–end. See also the Note (below) on 'The Babylonian Job'.

II

THE SATAN

THE Satan is one of 'the sons of Elohim', i.e. a member of the group which includes all supernatural beings. See 2 Kings ix. 1 (prophets), Ecclesiastes i. 13 (men), the Hebrew of Isaiah lx. 10 (foreigners), etc. All such groups are both comprehensive and exclusive, in- cluding all within the particular denomination, and excluding all others. See in the New Testament, Ephesians ii. 2, 'the sons of disobedience'; Romans

viii. 14, those who stand in a special relation to God and know it, having the Witness of the Spirit.

In Job no distinction (e.g. moral) is made other than supernatural as against human. All are ministers of Jehovah and His courtiers. It has been suggested that some are national 'patron saints' (Daniel x. 13, etc.; Isaiah xxiv. 21), but Daniel is second century B.C. and Isaiah xxiv–xxvii is probably early third century B.C. (the time of the Seleucids and the Ptolemies). Job is *c.* 400 B.C. The Satan has a roving commission on earth, the rest probably no particularized function.

The Satan has not yet achieved a personal name, only a functional one. He is God's Inspector-of-man on earth, and man's adversary in heaven. His duty is to detect evil-doers on earth, and in heaven to oppose their claims to righteousness. The word *satan* means 'adversary': cf. 1 Samuel xxix. 4; 1 Kings xi. 14; Psalm cix. 6; and especially Matthew xvi. 23 and Numbers xxii. 22 *ff.* In Job the Satan is already cynical, disbelieving, even on God's testimony, that Job is disinterestedly good. The character is as yet largely undeveloped, but the two main characteristics are there. He is *diabolos* (accuser) and *peirazon* (tempter). These two ideas are to be noted in the development of the character. In the somewhat earlier Zechariah iii, he falsely accuses Jeshua (cf. Septuagint Esther vii. 1, where Haman is a *diabolos*, a *false* accuser. This is the tendency of the word in later classical Greek, and even in the *Apology*). Later, the word becomes a proper name, and in 1 Chronicles xxi (contrast with 2 Samuel xxiv. 1) Satan is the adversary, not of man, but of God Himself. Here also

16

he has become the Tempter, enticing the pious man against God to his ruin.

Further development is outside the Old Testament. In the *Book of Enoch* (from 180 to 64 B.C.) Satan rules the counter-kingdom of evil (liii. 3), and under his authority there are Satans who existed even before the angels fell (Genesis vi). Their functions are to tempt men to evil (lxix. 4, 6), to accuse them (xl. 7), and finally to punish those who fall (liii. 3, etc.). In the Apocrypha, see the following passages: Ecclesiasticus xxi. 27; Wisdom ii. 24, the beginning of the identification with the serpent of Genesis iii; Tobit iv. 8, etc., Asmodaeus the evil spirit. The Satan-serpent appears in *The Secrets of Enoch*, in the Jewish Targums and Midrashes, and thence in Christian tradition. Various other identifications have been made: e.g. the Azrael of Leviticus xvi. 7–28 is the demon of the waste-places, who in Enoch x. 8 is he that 'taught all unrighteousness on earth'. The scape-goat thus is paid to the Devil. The New Testament has the developed Jewish horde of Satan and his satellites, with elemental powers of earth and air, personal agencies of a dark supernatural world which is antagonistic to God. The idea of Satan as Anti-Christ belongs properly to the development of the Creation-myth, where Rahab becomes the personification of Evil.

Attempts have been made to see Persian influence in the development of the idea of Satan. Certainly the apocalyptic ideas of post-exilic Jewry are due largely to Zoroastrian influence, i.e. successive ages of the world's history, the last great fight between Ahura-Mazda (Ormuzd) and Angra-Mainyu (Ahriman), though all were transformed by native Jewish ethical and religious ideas. There is a natural Hebrew development, both of Satan and of dualism, as the problem of evil and suffering steadily grows more acute, but both were reinforced by the dualism and the demonology of the farther East.

III

LIFE AFTER DEATH

EARLY belief was indefinite, with a general supposition that a man joined his ancestors, sleeping with the clan in a common burial ground, and perhaps having some sort of communion with them. For the former, Genesis xv. 15, xxv. 8, xlvii. 30, xlix. 29; for the latter, there is evidence in the excavations of ancient sites, Lachish, Moresheth, Megiddo, Bethshemesh, and so forth, that lamps and food were deposited in tombs and on graves. All was shadowy and vague, but the ghosts of the departed were recognizable, 1 Samuel xxviii. 14 (cf. xv. 27), and they lived as they had lived on earth, though languidly and without *nephesh* (vigour, appetite, energy, life-force), Isaiah xiv. 9; Ezekiel xxxii. 17–32.

In pre-exilic times and in early post-exilic times, this traditional belief in Sheol grew more dismal rather than joyful, and only the weary and prisoners hope for it, Job iii. 11–19. Sheol was deep down in the earth, a great cavern, none knew how vast or deep. The word is sometimes used in a purely geographical

18

sense, equalling the lowest depths of earth, Amos ix. 2; Isaiah vii. 11. Often it is a synonym for death, Isaiah xxviii. 15; Hosea xiii. 14; Habakkuk ii. 5; Numbers xvi. 31–33 (J). It is equal to Abaddon (the place of the lost), Job xxvi. 6, xxviii. 22; or to *Shachath* ('pit', not 'corruption'), Job xvii. 14. In this vasty cavern existed the Rephaim (Job xxvi. 5), the shades, similar to the *manes* of earlier Roman beliefs. (Note that these Rephaim are distinct from those of Genesis xiv. 5, etc., who were the ancient inhabitants of Canaan. Og King of Bashan was the last of them. Where Septuagint does not transliterate, it has 'giants' or 'Titans'.) In Sheol none can praise God, and all desire is dead. They are without God, who remembers them no longer, though He knows where the gates are (Job xxxviii. 17). The references are Psalms xxxi. 12 (Hebrew 13), lxxxviii. 4 *f.* (5 *f.*), 10–12 (11–13); Isaiah xxxviii. 18 (Hezekiah's tragic prayer), etc., and in Job the following: iii. 13–26, vii. 7–10, x. 21 *f.*, xiv. 1 *f.*, xiv. 13 (geographical), xiv. 14 (question asked, but not answered), xvi. 22, xvii. 13–16, xxi. 13, xxi. 32 *f.*, xxiv. 19 *f.*

Indications in the Old Testament of any real life after death are few. Isaiah xxvi. 19 (early third century) speaks of a heavenly dew which will reanimate the corpses of dead Israelites; Daniel xii. 2 (second century) refers to a resurrection of some good and some bad. Some have seen a reference in Psalm cxxxix. 7–12, and another in Psalm lxxiii. 24 *f.* In each case the reference is geographical. The Hebrew refers to 'the heavens', and the argument is valid only in the English versions. Further, *kabod* (glory) means honour and prosperity in this life, and not 'heavenly bliss'. Isaiah liii. 8–12 refers to life after death only if the Servant is regarded as an individual, if an emended text is used (e.g. Duhm's), and if it is not remembered that Death is a figure for the Exile (cf. Ezekiel xxxvii).

There remains Job xix. 25–7, which in the English A.V. refers to a resurrection life. 'Though worms destroy this body' is due to the Vulgate and bears no relation to the Hebrew Text, and similarly 'at the latter day'. The interpretation has been fostered by the popularity of Handel's *Messiah*. Neither Peake, nor Gray, nor Oesterley and Robinson see here any reference to a future life, though the tendency is to think of a momentary vision vouchsafed to Job after his death. A variant of this is Bruston's suggestion that Job is describing a present vision and sees by faith (cf. Hebrews xi). The passage is difficult and may be partly corrupt. Budde and Kautzsch understand it to mean a vindication in this life, which Job himself will see before he dies. This, in our view, is the most satisfactory solution.

In Ecclesiastes the writer rejects the idea of life after death: iii. 20 *f*., viii. 10, ix. 1–6. Ben Sirach holds to the traditional Sadducaean doctrine of Sheol, but the Pharisaic belief survived and is found in the New Testament.

Certain factors in the later development need to be pointed out. There is no doctrine anywhere in the Bible of the Immortality of the Soul in the sense that there is a part of man's nature which by its own right is immortal. This idea belongs to traditional Christianity, but it is non-Biblical. It comes from the Greeks. The Biblical doctrine is the Resurrection of the Body, the phrase of the Creeds. The dead (either those in Christ or all, some to condemnation) are raised up by the Will and Power of God. The idea of the resuscitation of the physical body is a crude and literal interpretation. Paul speaks of two kinds of bodies for man, a physical and a spiritual. In our modern categories, this use of the Greek *soma* means 'identity'. In the Fourth Gospel 'eternal life' (*zoe*) begins when a man is born of water and the Spirit. Physical life (*bios*) ceases at death. It should also be remembered that to a large extent the idea of life after death is associated in the New Testament with life on a transformed earth in the New Age of apocalyptic ideas.

IV

VARIOUS SHORT NOTES

1. *The Land of Uz*, i. 1. Probably south-east of Palestine, in or near Edom, Genesis xxxvi. 28; Lamentations iv. 21; Jeremiah xxv. 21–3. Eliphaz came from Edom, Genesis xxxvi. 11, 16, 31–4; Amos i. 11 *f.*; Habakkuk iii. 3, etc. There is a traditional connection between wisdom and Edom; cf. Jeremiah xlix. 7. See also the reference to Ram in 1 Chronicles ii. An alternative places Uz in the Aram-naharaim country, east of the Euphrates, Genesis x. 23, xxii. 21. Bildad the Shuhite may have come from south of Carchemish on the Euphrates, Genesis xxv. 2. For Buz, see Genesis xxii. 21.

2. *Shaddai*, v. 17, plus thirty times. Elsewhere in

the Old Testament only seventeen times, of which six are in P, two in the JE poem, Numbers xxiv. 4, 16, two in Ruth, and the *El Shaddai* of Genesis xlix. 25, an archaism, stated to be the ancient Name known to the Patriarchs, Exodus vi. 3 (P). Hence its use in Job. The Rabbinic explanation is 'the all-sufficient', and so Aquila, Symmachus and Theodotion. This is obtained by splitting it into two words. Septuagint and Vulgate mostly translate 'almighty' from the original sense of the root *shadad* as 'over-powerer'. This is the traditional English interpretation, and it is the best, though the actual meaning is uncertain. Other conjectures are 'my sovereign Lord' (Hoffman, on the basis of Phoenician inscriptions), 'rain-giver' (Robertson Smith, root *shadah*, pour forth), 'mountain' (Assyrian *shadu*), and 'the strong one' (Syriac, twelve times).

3. *The Helpers of Rahab*, ix. 13. This is a reference to the Creation-myth. In the Mesopotamian variant, Tiamat, the monster of the Under-sea or Primeval Ocean, recovers from the first defeat of the chthonic (under-world) gods, finds a new husband in a god named Kingu, and bears him a brood of monsters, 'the helpers of Tiamat'. When the hero-god (Marduk in sixth-century Babylon, but the hero-god varies from city to city, Jehovah being the Hebrew Hero) attacks her, her helpers flee, and she is left alone to meet the onset of the angry god. She is defeated. Some said she was slain, and divided into two parts, of which one was made into the sky, and the other into the earth. Others said she was tied round the inverted bowl of the sky to prevent it falling down on the earth. Yet others said she was bound back

a prisoner, lest she (the Mighty Deep) should over-flood the created earth, and bring back the primeval Chaos. Alternatively she was fastened down in the depths of the sea, and 'when the waves thereof roar', she is striving to break her bonds. Some said she was shattered in pieces and her head(s) broken, but all sorts of varied details describe her fate. The name Tiamat survives in the Hebrew *tehom*, 'the vasty deep' (i.e. the Primeval Ocean), Genesis i. 2, 7. The Hebrew name of the monster is Rahab (which also means pride; cf. Job ix. 13, A.V.). The Hebrews made her the Oppressor of Israel, the Enemy of God. Egypt is Rahab, and Babylon, and Nebuchadrezzar (Jeremiah li. 34, which is decisive for the Book of Jonah); Rahab is the new 'Babylon', Rome, and the great beast which comes up out of the sea. The references in Job are ix. 13, xli. 34, xl. 15–24 (cf. 2 Esdras of the Apocrypha, vi. 49–52), vii. 12, xxxviii. 8–11, xli. 8. Elsewhere some of the references are Amos ix. 3; Psalms xxiv. 2, xxix. 10 (not Noah's flood), lxxiv. 12–17, xciii, civ. 26; Exodus xv. 5; Isaiah xxx. 7; Ezekiel xxix. 3–6, xxxii. 2–8; Isaiah li. 9–11. lii. 7 *f*.; Revelation xiii. 1. This is the origin of Anti-Christ. The idea of the last great fight is borrowed from Zoroastrian traditions.

4. *Redeemer* (*Go'el*), xix. 25. The root *ga'al* is used for ensuring the return of property to the original owner, or, in the case of death, seeing to it that the deceased gets the rights which were his in life. The root *padah* refers to obtaining (by payment) that which was not the receiver's. E.g. vows can be redeemed (*ga'al*), but the first-born was originally God's, and therefore the word is *padah*. For the redemption

23

out of Egypt the word is *padah*, because God chose
Israel at Sinai, but for the release from Babylon it is
ga'al. So *Go'el* means Vindicator, the one who sees
that the helpless one gets his rights. One use of the
word is next-of-kin, cf. Ruth iii. 13, but this meaning
is by no means essential.

5. *Ophir*, xxii. 24, xxviii. 16. The ocean-going
(Tarshish) fleets of Hiram and Solomon traded to
Ophir, setting out from Eziongeber in the Gulf of
Aqabah (N.-E. arm of Red Sea), 1 Kings x. 22, etc.
It was a three years' journey, and they returned with
gold, silver, ivory, apes, peacocks, etc. The location
is uncertain. (i) Arabic, though exact locality varies,
the most satisfactory being south-eastern, in the region
of the Gulfs of Oman and Persia. These parts were
famous for gold in late classical times: cf. Diodorus
Siculus, Strabo, and Pliny. All ancients and most
moderns prefer this. Not all the products came from
there, but there were doubtless trade-routes to India
and the east. *Qophim* (apes), *algummim* (sandal-wood),
and *tukkiyyim* (peacocks) are all Sanskrit words, and
some of them are in use on the Malabàr Coast to-day.
(ii) Punt, i.e. the Ethiopian coast of the Red Sea and
the opposite coast of Arabia. Not far enough away,
and not famous enough for gold. (iii) East Coast of
Africa, perhaps as far down as opposite Madagascar,
though some say farther north. It is alleged that this
was the Punt of the Egyptians, notably the ruins of
Zimbabwe discovered in 1871 in Mashonaland,
between the Zambesi and the Limpopo. Phoenician
sailors knew this coast in ancient times. This identification is attractive, but the first is most likely.

6. *Mazzaroth*, xxxviii. 32. R.V. 'ordinances', but

in the margin 'the twelve signs of the zodiac'. Probably the same as the *mazzaloth* of 2 Kings xxiii. 5 (*l* and *r* are easily confused, e.g. Guadalcanal and Guadalcanar). Probably an Assyrian loan-word, 'station, abode'; cf. Syriac *mazzele* (mansions of the moon). Others think of particular constellations, e.g. Michaelis, Ewald suggested the Corona Borealis, or both the Crowns, Northern and Southern. Syriac here says 'the Wain'. All identifications are doubtful. Even the Bear of xxxviii. 32 is doubtful, some interpreting to be 'the Hen and her chickens' (Pleiades), so Targum. Similar doubts extend to the list of ix. 9.

7. *Wisdom*, xxviii. In this poem Wisdom is regarded as something concrete, which God alone knows and has searched out. It is not clearly stated what or who Wisdom is, but apparently the author thought of it as something in the nature of the great plan of creation and existence, the secret of all created things. God alone knows how all things cohere and according to what plan they work. Man's wisdom (i.e. knowledge of the way to live) is limited to worshipping God in humble fear and doing what is right. The picture of Wisdom, in so far as it is described at all, stops short of such a personification as that in Proverbs viii–ix. 6. This latter has been supposed to have its origin in one of the six Amesha-Spentas, the 'immortal holy ones' of Zoroastrian thought, particularly Armaiti (piety) whom Plutarch identified with the Greek Sophia. Rankin finds a closer analogy with Asha (Right Law), who, amongst other common characteristics, dwelt in a house with seven pillars.

8. *The Babylonian Job*. This is the story of Tabi-utul-bel, found transcribed from a more ancient text, in

the library of Asshur-bani-pal (668–626 B.C.). He was rich and suddenly became poor. He describes his sufferings at great length, and discusses the ways of God with man. The differences lie in the innocence of Job and the uncertainty in this respect of the Babylonian sufferer. He may have done something amiss, and he seeks to find out what it is. The general judgement of scholars is that this represents an insuperable difference. Another is that there is no dialogue, and no variation between prose and verse. For our part, we would point out, that if there was a stage when the present Book of Job was limited to prologue, epilogue, Job's soliloquy, Jehovah's speech and Job's subsequent recantation (as we have suggested above), then the difference between the two stories is negligible.

V

OTHER STUDIES

THERE are various other studies for which little more than a careful reading of the actual text is required. It is not the purpose of this little manual to discuss such subjects, but only such as require books not easily accessible. Such subjects are (i) the conception(s) of the Nature of God, especially as compared with the monotheism of Second-Isaiah, (ii) the various answers to the problem of suffering and the allied problem of retribution, (iii) the literary value of the Book, (iv) the relation to the Deuteronomist theory of retribution, (v) is Job a personification of Israel in Exile?

The best books in English are the commentaries by Peake (*Century Bible*) and Driver-Gray (*I.C.C.*). Also Peake, *The Problem of Suffering in the Old Testament* (Holborn Press), H. Wheeler Robinson, *The Cross of Job* (S.C.M., 1s.), J. E. McFadyen, *The Problem of Pain* (James Clarke, 6s. net). Two general books on Wisdom literature are useful: H. Ranston, *The Old Testament Wisdom Books and Their Teaching* (Epworth Press, 1930), and O. S. Rankin, *Israel's Wisdom Literature* (T. and T. Clark, 1936).

Printed in Great Britain by
The Camelot Press Ltd., London and Southampton